The

SUMMER
OLYMPICS

Published by Creative Education, Inc.
123 South Broad Street, Mankato, MN 56001

Designed by Rita Marshall with the help of Thomas Lawton
Cover illustration by Rob Day, Lance Hidy Associates

Photography by Allsport, Berg & Associates,
Black Star, Brooks & Vankirk, Globe Photos,
Spectra-Action, Wide World Photos

Printed in the United States

Library of Congress Cataloging-in-Publication Data

McGuire, William.
  The Summer Olympics/by William McGuire.
    p. cm.
    ISBN 0-88682-318-8
    1. Olympics—History. I. Creative Education, Inc.
(Mankato, Minn.) II. Title
GV 721.5.M399 1990
796.48—dc20   90-34650
                                                  CIP

The SUMMER OLYMPICS

WILLIAM McGUIRE

CREATIVE EDUCATION INC.

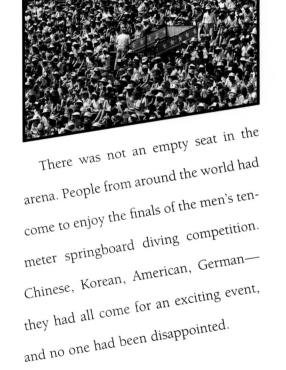

There was not an empty seat in the arena. People from around the world had come to enjoy the finals of the men's ten-meter springboard diving competition. Chinese, Korean, American, German— they had all come for an exciting event, and no one had been disappointed.

A young Chinese athlete had just executed a near-perfect dive to take a strong lead, and the crowd was buzzing. One competitor remained. Only one diver with only one chance to take the lead. A hush swept over the crowd as many of the spectators moved to the edge of their seats.

As the defending champion and winner of three previous gold medals, Greg Louganis had been expected to win. Now, as he eyed the end of the diving board, almost no one thought it was possible. Tension filled the air. Louganis, however, stared straight ahead, concentrating on his final dive. It was the most difficult one in his program, and it had to be perfect.

As he moved forward on the diving board, the crowd became as still as the water below. All the excitement and drama of Olympic competition seemed to be captured in this one great moment.

The gold medal

THE ANCIENT OLYMPICS

Throughout the years, the Olympic Games have produced many memorable occasions. The 1988 men's springboard competition is just one example. There have been many others. Johnny Weissmuller's record-setting swimming performance in 1924, Fanny Blankers-Koen's four gold medals in 1948, and the Soviet Union's victory over the United States in the 1972 men's basketball competition are just several more.

For just how many years the Olympics have been providing these wonderful memories no one is certain. Most experts agree that the Games probably began as early as 1300 B.C. Yet, it was not until 776 B.C. that the first Olympic champion was noted in the record books.

In the 1988 games, Greg Louganis knew that his last dive would have to be perfect.

The Games at that time were held at Olympia in the Greek city of Elis. Like all Greek sporting events of that period, the Olympics were only a small part of a large religious festival. The athletic portion was so small that in 776 B.C. there was only one sporting event—a footrace.

The contest was held on a track about 35 yards wide. The racing length was one stade, a distance of about 210 yards. About fifty participants came from more than twelve Greek cities to compete. In what we can only imagine as a close race, Coroebus of Elis, a cook by profession, was the winner. It was the first recorded great moment in Olympic history, and Coroebus was an Olympic champion.

During the ancient Olympics, the athletic competitions were held in amphitheatres.

Olympic competition in the ancient era was not much different than it is today. Athletes, with the help of coaches, underwent extended and very difficult training programs. Eventually, competitors became full-time specialists to increase their chances of winning. The honor and prestige, not to mention the unlimited benefits, of being an Olympic champion were tremendous. It was an environment that produced many great moments.

The first-ever event, the footrace, became an Olympic tradition.

In time, thousands of spectators gathered at Olympia to witness the fierce competition. As the popularity of the Games grew, so did the number of events. Wrestling, horse racing, boxing, and chariot racing were just a few of the contests added. Eventually, the Games even included events for fully armed soldiers, for heralds, and for trumpeters.

Unfortunately, over time, this atmosphere and the spirit of competition were lost. By A.D. 394, the Olympics had become so corrupt that the Christian Emperor Theodosius I banned the event.

The modern Olympic Games were established in 1896.

A MODERN REVIVAL

For nearly 1,500 years, the ruins and the memories of great Olympic moments remained buried beneath the earth. It was not until 1878, when a team of German archaeologists excavated the remains of the ancient Olympic site, that the Olympic spirit was revived.

Inspired by the work of the archaeologists, French nobleman Baron Pierre de Coubertin began to organize the renewal of the Olympic Games. It was his hope that a worldwide competition could be held to promote goodwill and harmony among nations. "Let us export our oarsmen, our runners, our fencers into other lands," de Coubertin remarked. "That is the true Free Trade of the future; and the day it is introduced into Europe the cause of Peace will have received a strong and new ally."

In 1896, de Coubertin's dream was realized and a new era of great Olympic moments began. In the first week of April, the first modern Olympic Games were officially opened by the king of Greece. Thirteen nations, sending nearly 300 representatives, gathered in Athens to take part in forty-two events and ten different sports.

Of all the various events held, the Greek spectators had the most interest in the marathon. According to legend, the first marathon runner was an Athenian soldier named Pheidippides, who ran the twenty-six miles from Marathon to Athens to bring the news of an Athenian victory in a war against Prussia. He delivered the message successfully, but the exhausting run killed him.

In Pheidippides's honor, the first Olympic marathon was held April 9, 1896. Seventeen runners gathered in Marathon to retrace his steps. Messengers riding horses and bicycles brought news of the race to a packed stadium crowd watching other events in Athens. The news wasn't good for the Greek fans at first; an Australian named Edwin Flack was leading the field.

After a time, an excited messenger rode into the stadium and ran up to the king and queen of Greece, who were seated in the royal box. Slowly, fans all around the stadium began shouting "El-leen! Elleen!," which means "A Greek! A Greek!" Within minutes, a Greek shepherd named Spiridon Louis entered the stadium to wild cheering. Two Greek princes rushed down to greet the runner and raced the final lap around the stadium with him. Spiridon Louis had become the first Greek Olympic champion in over 1,500 years.

Despite the success of the first modern Olympics in Athens, the Olympic movement took some time to gather momentum. By 1912, however, the Olympic Games in Stockholm attracted twenty-eight nations and over 2,500 competitors. Among these 2,500 athletes, one supremely trained individual stood above all others. His name was Jim Thorpe.

The versatile native American athlete provided the spectators with a glimpse of the modern Olympics' first outstanding individual star. Displaying his many skills, Thorpe won both the five-event pentathlon and the ten-event decathlon. Both test an athlete's ability in a combination of running, jumping, and throwing events. And no one had greater all-around athletic ability than Jim Thorpe.

"Sir, you are the greatest athlete in the world," commented Swedish King Gustav V at the medal ceremonies. The more than 20,000 people in attendance agreed. Their wild applause and cheers were deafening. A humble Thorpe could only respond, "I can't realize how one fellow could have so many friends."

King Gustav was one of the spectators thrilled by Thorpe's performance.

Yet the friendships made and nurtured by the Olympics were torn apart from 1914 to 1918 by the destruction of World War I. The Olympic movement, strengthened by sportsmen like Jim Thorpe, survived the war, and in 1920, less than two years after peace was declared, the Olympic Games were opened in Antwerp, Belgium.

The year 1920 marked not only the return of the Olympics but also the beginning of a golden age of athletes. From Antwerp to Berlin, great performers made their mark on Olympic history. Some of the most remarkable accomplishments came from the Finnish participants. Their domination of Olympic middle- and long-distance running events was complete. Of these individuals, the greatest was the "Flying Finn."

14

The men's hurdles are another popular track-and-field event.

There had never been a long-distance runner like Paavo Nurmi. The tall, quiet, blond athlete was all business. Once on the track he paid little attention to his opponents. All of his concentration was focused on his task and the stopwatch he always carried with him.

Paavo Nurmi

In Antwerp, Nurmi lost his first Olympic event, the 5,000-meter run. That, however, would be one of the few races the "Flying Finn" would lose in the next nine years. Among his many accomplishments were two gold medals in Antwerp and an amazing five gold medals in eight days at the Paris Olympics in 1924.

Nothing seemed to bother this great competitor. Nurmi was not even upset when he learned that the finals of the 1,500-meter race in Paris were scheduled less than an hour before the 5,000-meter finals. He won the first race in an Olympic record time of 3:53.6, then rushed to the locker room to rest. Fifty-five minutes later, Nurmi was back on the track for the second contest. His opponents tried to tire him out by setting a very fast pace at the beginning, but Nurmi stayed with them. He passed everyone at the halfway mark and never looked back as he recorded another record-breaking performance.

Before Nurmi's Olympic career was over, he would win two more gold medals in the 1928 Olympics. Altogether the "Flying Finn" competed in three Olympics and took home nine gold medals. It was an extraordinary string of performances by an extraordinary competitor.

While Paavo Nurmi displayed his endurance, the title of "fastest man in the world" is reserved for the winner of the

The 100-meter dash determined the "fastest man in the world."

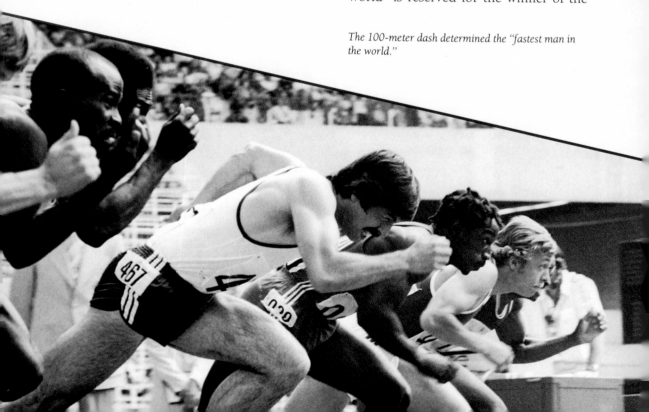

100-meter dash. The event usually produces close contests and occasionally great debates, but there was no question who the fastest man and the best all-around Olympic athlete in the world was at the 1936 Games in Berlin, Germany. That honor belonged to Jesse Owens.

Owens and other black athletes at the Berlin Olympics were under extreme pressure. German dictator Adolf Hitler had proclaimed that his white German athletes were superior to any black athlete at the Games. At the beginning of the Games, the hostile atmosphere intimidated Owens. In his first event, the long jump, Owens fouled on his first two attempts. Another foul and he would not qualify for the finals.

Watching Owens struggle was his German opponent, Luz Long. Before Jesse's final attempt, Long approached Owens. He quietly informed Jesse that most of the Germans did not share Hitler's hatred. A more relaxed Owens easily qualified for the finals on his next attempt. Later that day, he outdueled Luz Long for the gold medal. "You can melt down all the medals and cups I have," commented Owens, "and they wouldn't be a plating on the twenty-four-carat friendship I felt for Luz Long."

Jesse Owens outdueled Luz Long (at right) for the gold medal.

The friendship with Long and the gold medal in the long jump were just the beginning of Jesse's success at the 1936 Olympics. He also won the 100- and 200-meter dashes and contributed to the United States' victory in the 400-meter relay race. Owens's fantastic achievements brought an end to the golden age of athletes—from the endurance of Nurmi to the speed of Owens, it had been a memorable period in Olympic history.

UNEQUALED PERFORMANCES

For forty years prior to the 1968 Olympics in Mexico City, the best long jumpers in the world had considered the distance of twenty-six feet to be a mark of success. It had taken more than twenty-five years for Jesse Owens's mark, set in the 1936 Olympics, of twenty-six feet eight inches to be broken. In Mexico City, no one imagined the record would be pushed any farther.

In 1984, Carl Lewis won gold medals in the same events Owens had in 1936.

Jesse Owens during the 1936 Olympics.

Among the athletes gathered to compete in the long jump was Bob Beamon. A six-foot-three twenty-two-year-old from South Jamaica, New York, Beamon was a talented but very inconsistent jumper.

After barely qualifying for the finals, Beamon needed a much-improved per-

Bob Beamon was a talented, but inconsistent, jumper.

formance to have any chance of winning an Olympic medal. There were seventeen athletes scheduled to compete, and Beamon was to jump fourth. The first three competitors committed fouls, and their jumps were disqualified. Bob Beamon was next.

As he stood at the beginning of the runway, Bob paused and collected his thoughts. Once mentally prepared, he tore down the runway and hit the take-off board perfectly. As he flew through the air and prepared to land, "he looked like a huge, limby frog," commented one reporter. "His legs were spread-eagled and arms were dangling between them. When he finally did land, he hit with so much velocity and so close to the end of the pit, that he bounced out on one hop."

At first, Beamon didn't realize how far he had leapt. When the measurement of 8.90 meters—or twenty-nine feet, two and one-half inches—was posted, Bob fell to the ground and kissed the earth. The jump was a new world record and nearly two feet farther than anyone had ever gone before. "It is one world record which may never be beaten," ex-Olympic champion and athletics expert Harold Abrahams commented.

Today, over twenty years later, the record remains. It is the oldest track record existing and proof that Bob Beamon's long jump in 1968 was one of the greatest moments in Olympic history.

Another historic performance occurred at the 1976 Olympics in Montreal, Canada. Before the 1976 Games, when people mentioned women's gymnastics, the immediate reaction was Olga Korbut. In 1972, in Munich, West Germany, Korbut gave several emotional performances that brought women's gymnastics into the international spotlight. Four years later, she was still considered by many to be the best female gymnast in the world. By the end of the 1976 Olympics, however, that would all change.

In the midst of Korbut and thousands of skilled athletes, a small fourteen-year-old Romanian girl stepped forward and gave a series of gymnastic performances that were unforgettable. With each of her brief routines, Nadia Comaneci made a lasting mark on Olympic history.

Her record was impressive—three gold medals, including the women's all-around competition, one silver, and one bronze medal. Her teammates and even her opponents were awed by her accomplishments. "Nadia is in a class all her own," remarked U.S. team manager Rod

Hill. "She could throw ten, twenty or thirty routines in one occasion and score 9.8 or better in each of them. I have seen her throw six consecutive bar routines," he continued, "and hit every one of them . . . she is fantastic."

Nadia received a perfect score of 10.0 on the uneven bars.

But the one moment that no one anticipated was one of her early performances on the uneven bars. From one move to the next, Nadia was in complete control. Her routine seemed effortless. After completing her dismount from the bars, Comaneci patiently waited for the score. Eventually, the scoreboard lit up. It registered 1.00.

The crowd was silent. How could the score be so low? Soon they would learn. The computer used to display the scores had only been programmed to record a score up to 9.99. Nadia had not received a 1.00 but a 10.0, the first perfect score in Olympic history. Everyone in attendance was amazed. Everyone that is, except Comaneci. "I knew it was flawless," she commented. "I have done it fifteen times before."

By the end of the Games, Comaneci would repeat this perfect performance five more times. Like Bob Beamon's long jump in 1968, it is an unequaled Olympic record.

Jubilant Olympic champions celebrated their winning performances.

Vassily Alexeyev

MORE SUMMER STARS

While tiny, graceful athletes like Nadia Comaneci were entertaining fans in the gymnastics events, two powerful giants established amazing winning streaks in weight lifting and boxing.

It's not unusual for a top weight lifter to raise a bar weighing nearly twice his weight over his head. But when the athlete weighs more than 300 pounds, like Russian Vassily Alexeyev, that's a lot to lift. In 1972, Alexeyev easily earned the title of "World's Strongest Man" by becoming the first Olympian to jerk a bar weighing more than 500 pounds from the ground to above his head. The "Russian Bear" repeated his gold-medal performance in 1976, outlifting his nearest competitor by thirty-five kilograms, nearly 80 pounds.

These athletes often lifted bars twice their own weight.

knockouts in the 1972 Olympics. Four years later, Stevenson continued his unbeaten streak at the Montreal Olympics. Not only did he defeat all his opponents; none of them even lasted the full three rounds against him. In the 1976 finals, he faced Mircea Simon of Romania. Simon dodged and ran away from Stevenson for the first two rounds. Stevenson caught up with Simon in the third round, however. He connected against Simon's jaw with such a powerful punch that the Romanian's trainers quickly threw a towel into the ring to halt the bout.

In 1980 in Moscow, two of Stevenson's opponents became the first ever to go the distance against him, but the Cuban champion won both bouts by decisions. He retired from Olympic competition as the only boxer to win three gold medals in the same weight division. Throughout his career, Stevenson remained an amateur. He turned down several multimillion-dollar offers to turn professional. "I wouldn't exchange my piece of Cuba," he commented, "for all the money they could give me."

Cuban boxer Téofilo Stevenson may not have been as big as Alexeyev, but he was both powerful and lightning quick. He demolished all opponents with

Teofilo Stevenson overwhelmed his opponents with his power.

These boxers shared the same competitive spirit as Teofilo Stevenson.

Like Téofilo Stevenson and other outstanding Olympic champions before him, Greg Louganis had provided spectators with many great performances throughout his Olympic career. Now, as he was about to attempt his final dive of his Olympic career, he knew it had to be his best.

As Louganis bounced on the end of the diving board, one could sense that this could be another great moment in Olympic history. After pushing off the board a second time, Louganis soared up and away from the platform.

In the air, he gracefully bent forward and began a series of difficult gymnastic maneuvers. Three and one-half flips and several spins later, his body quickly dropped toward the water. Now fully extended, Louganis sliced quietly into the pool with just a slight hint of a splash. Beautiful!

The crowd roared, and Louganis emerged from the pool with a smile of pure joy. He had done it; he was once again an Olympic champion.

With another championship in sight, Louganis gracefully spun toward the water.